JOURNEY THROUGH
Italy

Colin Clark

Troll Associates

Library of Congress Cataloging-in-Publication Data

Clark, Colin, (date)
  Journey through Italy / by Colin Clark;
illustrated by Robert Burns ... [et al.].
    p.   cm
  Includes index.
  Summary: Describes some distinct features of
life in Italy and, in particular, such cities as
Rome, Florence, Genoa, Milan, Venice, and
Pompeii.
  ISBN 0-8167-2763-5 (lib. bdg.)
  ISBN 0-8167-2764-3 (pbk.)
  1. Italy—Juvenile literature.   [1. Italy]
I. Burns, Robert, ill.   II. Title
DG417.C55   1994
945—dc20   91-46174

Published by Troll Associates
© 1994 Eagle Books

Edited by Neil Morris and
Kate Woodhouse
Design by Sally Boothroyd
Picture research by Jan Croot

Illustrators: Martin Camm: 4, 5; Frank
Nichols: 10, 24-25; Ian Thompson: 4-5.

Pictures credits: Bridgeman Art Library:
11, 20-21; Clive Barda: 16/17; Colorsport: 7, 16;
Chris Fairclough: 6, 14, 17; Susan Griggs: 23;
Hutchison Library: 8, 11, 13; Hutchison
Library/J. Davey: 9, 10; Hutchison Library/
John Egan: 18; Hutchison Library/Robert
Francis: 26-27; Hutchison Library/Michael
Dunne: 30; Hutchison Library/Christine
Pemberton: 6-7, 13, 28; Rex Features Ltd: 26;
Spectrum: 12-13, 18, 19, 20, 20-21, 22; ZEFA: 9,
14-15, 24-25, 26-27, 29.

Printed in the U.S.A.
10 9 8 7 6 5 4 3 2 1

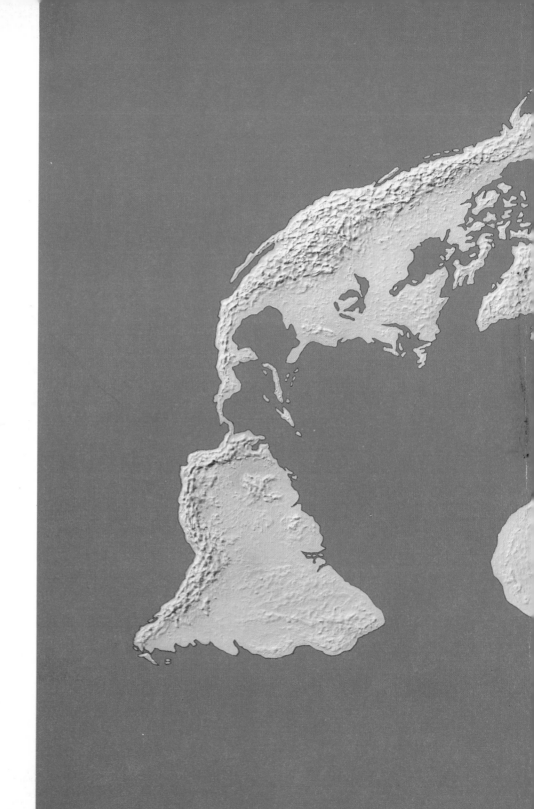

CONTENTS

Italy

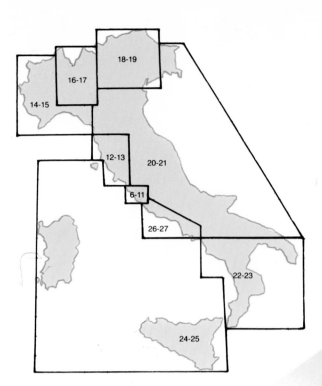

wolf

Animals of Italy
Dolphins can often be seen in the seas around Italy. Wolves still roam the lonely, mountainous parts of Italy, keeping as far away from people as they can.

In this book we take a fascinating journey through Italy. The numbers on the small map above show which pages deal with which parts of Italy.

KEY FACTS

Area: 116,314 sq. mi. (301,252 sq. km.)

Population: 57,505,000

Capital: Rome 2,816,000 people

Other major cities: Milan 1,464,000; Naples 1,203,000; Turin 1,012,000

Highest mountain: Gran Paradiso 13,323 ft. (4,061 m)

Longest river: Po 405 mi. (652 km.)

Largest lake: Lake Garda 142 sq. mi. (370 sq. km.)

dolphin

Alps
Lake Maggiore
Lake Como
Varese
Milan
LOMBARDY
Turin
Verona
Po
Venice
Trieste

Genoa
Cinque Terre
EMILIA
Bologna
ROMAGNA
Pisa
Arno
Florence
TUSCANY
Siena
Assisi
UMBRIA
ELBA
Tiber
ROME
ABRUZZI
CAMPANIA
Naples
Vesuvius
Pompeii
Sorrento
Positano
Amalfi
APULIA
BASILICATA
SARDINIA
ADRIATIC SEA
CALABRIA
MEDITERRANEAN SEA
Palermo
Mt Etna
SICILY

The Italian flag has green, white, and red vertical stripes. It is based on the flag designed by Napoleon for his army's Italian legion. The Italian national anthem was written in 1848 by the poet Goffredo Mameli. He was only 22 when he died in 1849 of wounds during the first war of Italian independence against Austria.

5

Welcome to Italy

Italy is a country of great natural beauty. Three-quarters of the country is mountainous, and about one-fifth is covered in forests. It is more than 1,000 miles (1,600 kilometers) from the Alps in the north to Sicily in the south. The country's long, narrow shape means that no place in Italy is more than 112 miles (180 kilometers) from the sea. The mainland coastline stretches for over 1,400 miles (2,300 kilometers), and much of it is very beautiful. The landscapes of Tuscany and Umbria, with their hills covered by cypress trees, olives, and vines, are known and loved by visitors from all over the world.

Italy has been one of the world's most popular tourist destinations for years. It is estimated that 8 million people come to see the city of Venice each year, and its own population is less than 80,000.

On the map, Italy looks like a leg in a high-heeled boot about to kick a ball – Sicily. At knee height there is another ball, Sardinia. This resemblance is appropriate, because soccer is a national passion for Italians!

◀ Italian ice cream is world famous. The Romans made water ices, and the explorer Marco Polo came across milk ices on his journey to China in the 13th century. It is thought that ice cream was first brought to Sicily by the Arabs and that the Sicilians added snow from Mount Etna. In Italian, an ice cream is a *gelato*.

▲ Soccer, or *futbol*, is a passion for Italians. This is a match between teams from Rome, or *Roma,* and Naples, or *Napoli.* Large crowds watch the major clubs every Sunday throughout the playing season. Many of the greatest soccer players from other countries are paid huge sums of money to play for the rich Italian clubs.

▲ Florence, *Firenze* in Italian, is the capital of the region of Tuscany. Between 1400 and 1550, it was the most important art center in the world. The skyline of its historic center is famous for the dome of its cathedral, or *duomo.* It was built in the mid-1400s, and seems to watch over today's city of 500,000 people.

The Italian people are colorful and dramatic, and they are warm and friendly to visitors. They care very much about style and fashion, and the evening promenade is an important social occasion in small villages and large cities alike.

The name Italy (*Italia*) comes from the Italic tribes who lived in the south in ancient times. The unit of currency is the *lira.* Rome is the capital, and we shall begin our journey there.

All roads lead to Rome

Rome is the center of Italy. It is a very old city. According to legend, it was founded by Romulus and Remus in 753 B.C. on the seven hills beside the Tiber River. In 133 B.C. Rome had a population of over a million. It was the world's first great city. By 1300, the population had shrunk to 20,000 and in 1870 it was only 220,000. Today, Rome has a population of nearly 3 million.

Rome was at the center of one of the world's greatest empires, which lasted from 27 B.C. to A.D. 476. The Roman Empire stretched from Scotland to Egypt, from the Atlantic Ocean to the Persian Gulf.

As you travel into Rome from the airport, you are reminded that you are entering the city of the Caesars, the emperors of ancient Rome. You see signs for the Via Appia, the Via Cassia, and the Via Aurelia, roads which were built by the ancient Romans and are still used today.

▼ When the Colosseum was opened in A.D. 80, the first spectacle lasted for a hundred days. The ancient Romans had bloodthirsty tastes. The shows that drew the crowds included gladiators, who were trained fighters, battling with each other or with wild beasts, and Christians being thrown to hungry lions. A legend says that when the Colosseum falls, Rome will fall.

All around the center of Rome are ancient buildings, monuments, statues, and fountains. Much of the water for these fountains comes through pipes or *aqueducts* built by the ancient Romans.

The traffic surrounding you tells you that you are also in a modern city. Visitors and Romans alike are surrounded by revving engines, squealing tires, and blaring horns. Driving in Italy is not for the faint-hearted!

◀ Some visitors find it difficult to adjust to driving in Rome. Narrow streets and fast-moving traffic make driving an adventure!

▼ The Trevi Fountain is one of Rome's most popular tourist attractions. It is said that if you throw a coin into it, you will return to Rome.

The Eternal City

Wherever you go in Rome, you are among people from other parts of the world. For more than 2,000 years, the city has attracted visitors. The ancient Romans were the first to call Rome, the center of their empire, "the Eternal City." Today it is not only the largest city in Italy and the country's capital, but also the center of the Roman Catholic Church. Rome is also a place of pilgrimage for Christians of all kinds, because two of the greatest saints, Peter and Paul, were put to death in Rome for their faith. Many Christians were killed in Rome in the first 200 years after Jesus Christ died, and their cemeteries, which are extensive underground vaults and galleries called *catacombs*, are still being uncovered today.

St. Peter's Basilica is the largest Christian church in the world. It is built over the place where St. Peter is said to have been martyred. St. Peter's is part of the Vatican. Inside the Vatican are thousands of works of art, including the Sistine Chapel whose ceiling was painted by the great sculptor and artist, Michelangelo. He took from 1508 to 1512 to complete this great work of art. It is said that, after so many years spent lying on his back, he could only read letters by holding them over his head.

Modern Italy was only formed in 1861 when many small states were united, so Rome is the capital of one of the youngest countries in Europe.

▶ The Vatican has an army, the Swiss Guards. Founded in 1505 as the Pope's personal bodyguard, these young soldiers are recruited exclusively in Switzerland. They wear bright, colorful uniforms which are said to have been designed by the great genius of the Renaissance, Michelangelo. Swiss Guards fought as mercenaries in various European armies from the 15th to the 19th centuries.

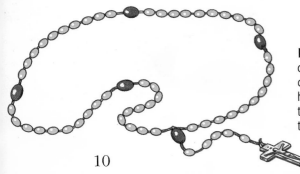

▶ St. Peter's Square, in front of the great church, is where crowds of pilgrims gather to hear the words of the head of the Roman Catholic Church, the Pope.

► For centuries the Vatican has been the center of the Roman Catholic Church and the home of the Pope. In 1929, it was recognized as an independent state inside Italy. Although it is only 109 acres (44 hectares), it contains the great church of St. Peter's and the Vatican palace and Museums. These are filled with priceless works of art. The Sistine Chapel is one of the most famous buildings. On its walls and ceiling, Michelangelo painted magnificent frescoes of the Creation and the Last Judgment.

The jewels of Tuscany

From Rome, you can travel north on Italy's most luxurious train, the *Settebello*. As you sit back in your seat, the train rushes you towards Tuscany, one of the largest of the country's 20 regions. The cities of Florence, Siena, and Pisa are the "three jewels of Tuscany."

Florence, the biggest of these cities, holds a unique place in history. It was here about 600 years ago that there was a rebirth, a *Renaissance*, in thinking about art, science, and learning. Today Florence is a bustling, traffic-filled city, with an historic center filled with workshops where leather goods, fabrics, and fine jewelry are made. The Arno River flows through the city, beneath the Ponte Vecchio, a bridge built in 1345 and lined with goldsmiths' shops. Each year a free-for-all soccer tournament is held in one of the main squares, the Piazza della Signoria. The teams, from the four quarters of the city, dress in medieval costume.

Centuries ago Siena and Florence were bitter enemies, and there is still rivalry between the cities. The focus of life in Siena is the fan-shaped Piazza del Campo, considered the most beautiful square in Italy. Twice each year the *Corso del Palio*, a bareback horse race, takes place here. It is a scene of magnificent pageantry.

Pisa is near the coast and was once a great sea power. Its chief glory is the Campo dei Miracoli, a grassy open area containing a magnificent cathedral, a baptistery, and the world-famous Leaning Tower.

► The *Palio* is not just for tourists, it is also a vital part of life today in Siena. The various districts, called *contrade*, are fierce rivals. Riders and their horses are blessed in churches before taking part in the race.

▲ Before the *Palio*, the flags of the different *contrade* are thrown in the air.

◄ The Leaning Tower of Pisa was built from 1173 to 1372. It started leaning after the first three stories were completed, and now tilts about 14½ feet (4.4 meters) from the vertical.

▼ San Gimignano, built on a hill between Florence and Siena, has hardly changed in over 500 years.

Coastal ports

From Pisa you can travel north along a coastline of sandy beaches and holiday resorts. Just inland lie the marble quarries that were begun in Roman times and are still working today. They supplied Michelangelo with the great blocks for his statues.

Further north, at Cinque Terre, the cliffs are so steep that some of the remote fishing villages are still unreachable by car. Vineyards are planted on the steep hillsides, and men have to be lowered on ropes from the clifftops to pick the grapes.

Italy is one of the world's top ten exporting countries and Genoa is its main port. It rivals Marseille in France as the most important port in the Mediterranean. For centuries, Genoa ruled the Mediterranean world, with colonies in the Crimea, Syria, and North Africa. The city was known as *La Superba*, "the Proud," until she was finally defeated by Venice in 1380. Genoa has a fascinating historic center but some visitors, overwhelmed by the maze of one-way streets and the constant traffic jams, never get to see it!

◀ Genoa is a busy, modern city and the capital of the region of Liguria, which includes the Italian Riviera. Christopher Columbus was born here, and so was Garibaldi, who led Italy's fight for freedom.

▲ Cinque Terre, the "Five Lands," is a collection of remote fishing villages along the Italian Riviera. They are built on cliffs so steep that only the sure-footed ever visit them!

Turin, an industrial center northwest of Genoa, is said to be the most French city in Italy. For many years it was the capital of the French province of Savoy. Nearby, in the Alpine valleys of the Val de Lys, the place names are all French, the people speak German, and yet you are in Italy!

The plains of Lombardy

The city of Milan lies in the fertile plain of Lombardy, east of Turin. It is a major center for fashion, industry, finance, and business. Milan is also Italy's most important railway junction.

Historically, the city has belonged to France, Spain, and Austria. It was founded about 400 B.C. by the Celts. Its cathedral can hold about 40,000 people. The painting of *The Last Supper* by Leonardo da Vinci is in another church in Milan. It was completed in 1497 and art restorers are working to prevent it from fading away completely. La Scala in Milan is one of the world's most famous opera houses.

▶ This ferry is crossing Lake Maggiore, one of the beautiful lakes in northern Italy. People come here from Milan to enjoy the wonderful scenery and fresh air, away from the rush and bustle of the city.

▲ Ferrari is one of the most famous makers of Italian cars. Their bright red racing cars are often winners in Grand Prix competitions.

▶ The auditorium of La Scala is as splendid as many of the operas performed on its stage. An evening at the opera is a great occasion.

The plains around Milan are the most fertile in northern Italy. They are irrigated by water from the Po River and from canals. There are up to eight cuts of hay a year, and rice is grown in paddy fields. The lakes Maggiore and Como are in the mountains north of Milan and are easy to reach. They are popular holiday resorts for Italians as well as people from all over Europe.

The Alps seem like a formidable barrier, closing Italy off from its northern neighbors. In reality, as you travel east from Milan, you come across many passes through the mountains. No less than 17 of the 23 main passes have been in use since ancient Roman times.

From Verona to Venice

Italy had the first superhighway in the world. In 1924 an *autostrada* was opened between Milan and Varese. Now superhighways serve the whole country, and one of the busiest runs east from Milan to Venice on the Adriatic Sea.

You could stop at Verona on the way. This ancient city has the best-preserved Roman amphitheater in the world, as well as Juliet's house with its balcony, made famous in Shakespeare's play, *Romeo and Juliet*.

North of Verona is the German-speaking part of Italy, known as Alto Adige and South Tyrol. It is a busy holiday area now, but in the First World War this was the front line in the struggle between Italy and Austria. The opposing armies fired at the overhanging snowfields, not at each other, and over 50,000 men were killed by avalanches.

Children going to school in Venice travel by water. The city is built on water and goods are transported by barge, while people use a water-bus or *vaporetto*. Venice has been a great city for 1,500 years, and for centuries it was the greatest sea power in the world.

▲ Verona was an important town in Roman times. Its magnificent amphitheater is used in summer for opera. It was also the home of Romeo and Juliet. You can still see the balcony from which, one moonlit night, Juliet cried: "O Romeo, Romeo, wherefore art thou, Romeo?"

◄ Venice is ideal for a carnival, because the streets are free from traffic! Masks are real works of art. Some people wear back-to-front costumes so it looks as if they are walking backwards!

▲ Venice is built on 118 small islands and criss-crossed by about 100 canals. One of the best ways to travel is by gondola, the traditional narrow boat. Every September there is a regatta on the Grand Canal. The highlight is a procession of historic boats manned by brightly costumed gondoliers.

It has thousands of close-packed houses in a maze of narrow streets, as well as magnificent churches and palaces. These are mainly alongside the canals that criss-cross the city. They have steps leading down to the water, where the famous *gondolas* are moored. The Grand Canal is the longest, at over two miles (three kilometers). For two weeks each spring, when Venice has its carnival, everyone takes to the streets and the canals in masks and costumes.

The land of St. Francis

From Trieste in the north to the "heel" of Italy, the east coast is about 750 miles (1,200 kilometers) long.

You can make the whole journey south by coach along the *autostrada*. But you would certainly wish to stop for a while in Bologna, an industrial and business center, where one of Europe's oldest and most famous universities was founded around A.D. 1000. It is said that you can find the best Italian food here in the Emilia-Romagna region. Along the coast are great stretches of sandy beaches and a number of seaside resorts.

In the center of Italy is its "green heart," the region of Umbria. This is the land of St. Francis, who was born in Assisi and died there in 1226. He is one of the best loved of all Christian saints, with his belief that people, animals and all of nature are creatures of God. He is the patron saint of animals and of Italy. Assisi itself has hardly changed from the Middle Ages. In the great church beneath which St. Francis is buried, there are a series of frescoes depicting his life. In those times the walls of churches acted as picture books for people who could not read.

Farther south is the mountainous Abruzzi region. At Cocullo there is a festival dating back to Roman times, in which a statue with live snakes draped on it is carried through the town.

▶ The Adriatic coast has miles of beaches, ideal for family holidays. Italians tend to limit their beach time to the hottest months of July and August, when their outgoing natures turn resorts, like Rimini, into lively places.

◀ Francis of Assisi is one of the most popular Christian saints, partly because of his love for animals. This picture was painted soon after his death in 1226 on a wall in the church named after him.

▼ The Umbrian landscape has rich valleys and gently rolling hills, many of them crowned by medieval towns. Everything seems quiet and peaceful, but there is always the threat of earthquakes.

The heel and the toe

In Apulia, the "heel" of Italy, you will find whitewashed houses with flat rooftops similar to those in the Middle East. You can see great cathedrals with Arab decorations on them. And there are circular stone huts with conical roofs called *trulli*. The origin of these simple houses is unknown, and some have pagan, magic symbols painted on them. Apulia is also an olive-growing area, producing vast amounts of olive oil.

Basilicata, Italy's "instep," is mostly mountainous and prone to earthquakes. Over 2,000 years ago, there was a great city on the coast, Metapontum, which was the home of Pythagoras, the famous Greek mathematician.

▼ The southern part of Italy is very poor, so many of the people earn money from tourism. People visit this area for its climate and scenery and for the contrast it offers to the north. You could imagine yourself in an Arab country in Apulia.

22

▲ Olives grow well in Apulia. They are picked and crushed to make fine olive oil that is exported throughout the world.

black squirrel

Calabria is the "toe" of Italy. It has over 370 miles (600 kilometers) of coastline, and most of the region is mountainous. In some towns in Calabria Albanian is still spoken, because refugees fled there from Albania in the Middle Ages. In some parts, wolves and black squirrels can be found.

In the time of ancient Rome, the south of Italy was rich. The north – the home of the barbarians – was poor. In modern Italy, the north and the middle of the country are rich and successful, while the south is poor and undeveloped. The Italian government has tried to change the situation with a development fund for the south, but much still needs to be done.

Italy's islands

From Calabria it is just a 30-minute ferry ride to Sicily. This is the largest island in the Mediterranean Sea, lying between Europe and Africa, and halfway between Gibraltar and Suez. Sicily is in the center of the sea that was once the center of the world.

Europe's largest active volcano dominates the east coast. Mount Etna is 11,122 feet (3,390 meters) high and has erupted over 200 times in the last 1,200 years. The climb to its summit is popular with tourists, especially at night when you can see the glowing lava in the crater.

Sicily's capital, Palermo, is a fascinating city. It is more Eastern than European in many ways, with buildings in Norman, Arabic, and Spanish styles. All of these peoples ruled Sicily at one time or another.

For years it has been the custom for Sicilian men to travel north in search of work or to emigrate to other countries because the island is so poor.

▼ The ferries from the mainland to Sicily are always busy, especially at holiday times. Sicilians who have had to go north to find work flock home to the island.

24

Sardinia lies 112 miles (180 kilometers) to the west of mainland Italy. Sardinians have their own language and customs. Their traditional costume, with the men in stocking caps and jerkins, is colorful and unusual. The island is sparsely populated, though it is home to two and a half million sheep!

The only other Italian island of any size is Elba, which is just off the coast of Tuscany and is a popular holiday destination.

◄ Cagliari is Sardinia's capital. People wearing traditional costumes travel there from all over the island for the annual Sacra de Sant'Efisio. Sardinia has thousands of prehistoric fortresses called *nuraghi*.

▼ It is about 87 miles (140 kilometers) around the base of Mount Etna. The volcano dominates the landscape of much of Sicily. When it erupts, which it does often, the lava usually flows slowly, so that the danger is to property, not people.

Naples and Pompeii

Naples is on the west coast, 136 miles (220 kilometers) south of Rome. For hundreds of years it was a royal capital. In the 16th and 17th centuries, Naples was the most populated capital in Europe, but in 1656 six out of ten of its inhabitants died of the Plague. Today it is plagued by overpopulation, unemployment, and poverty. It has many narrow, old streets filled with lively and energetic Neopolitans.

There are also many fine parts to the city. Its setting is one of outstanding beauty. Naples lies in the center of a wide-curving bay with mountains behind. The massive purple pyramid of the Vesuvius volcano dominates the view.

The most recent eruption of Vesuvius occurred in 1944. In A.D. 79 there was a great eruption that buried the Roman city of Pompeii under a thick layer of volcanic debris. You can walk around the excavated ruins of Pompeii and see exactly how ordinary Romans lived almost 2,000 years ago.

▲ Pompeii was buried so suddenly when Vesuvius erupted that its people were found, centuries later, lying where they fell.

◄ Naples is Italy's third largest city. Its setting is so beautiful that there is an old saying "See Naples and die," meaning there is nothing lovelier left to see in the world.

The whole area around Naples, called Campania, is full of exceptionally beautiful places. On the Amalfi peninsula to the south, picture-postcard towns such as Sorrento, Positano, and Amalfi cling to the sides of cliffs overlooking the blue sea.

You will have so many different things to remember at the end of your Italian journey: ancient monuments, works of art, magnificent buildings, beautiful scenery . . . and the colorful, friendly Italians themselves.

◄ The little resort of Amalfi, with only 6,500 inhabitants, was one of the great Mediterranean sea powers in the Middle Ages. Tourists flock to it and use it as a base for visiting places like Sorrento and Capri.

Fact file

Language

Italian is the language of almost everyone in Italy, although the regional dialects vary enormously. There are many German-speaking Italians in the northeast, and small groups elsewhere speaking Greek, Albanian, and Catalan, which is a form of Spanish. Italian is closer to Latin than any other language, and the Italian spoken by educated people in Tuscany, especially in Florence, is considered to be the standard. Say it in Italian!

(hi) hello	ciao!
goodbye	arrivederci
please	per favore
thank you	grazie
you're welcome	prego

Religion

The overwhelming majority of Italians are Roman Catholics.

Modern Italy

Italy is one of the youngest countries in Europe. It was founded as a monarchy in 1861, and in 1946 it became a democratic republic. The head of state is the president, who is elected for seven years. The country is divided into 20 regions. The regions are divided into provinces, and the provinces into communes.

Automobiles

Italy is a world leader in the design and manufacture of cars. Names such as Alfa Romeo, Bugatti, Ferrari, Fiat, Lancia, and Maserati have played an important part in the history of cars and auto racing. Fiat is one of the largest motor vehicle manufacturers in the world.

Sports

Soccer is the most popular sport in Italy, and leading players from all over the world play for Italian clubs. Every major city has its top professional team, while Rome, Milan, Turin, and Genoa each have two first-class teams. Another important sport is cycling and the Tour of Italy, the *Giro d'Italia,* attracts the finest international riders. Many Italian children learn to ski at an early age, and there are ski resorts down the whole length of Italy, from the Alps to Sicily. Basketball, baseball, and tennis are also very popular.

◄ A gondolier waiting for a passenger to take around Venice. Traveling by gondola is one of the best ways to see this unique city.

Independent states

Italy is unusual because it has two independent states, Vatican City and San Marino, within its borders.

Vatican City is the world's smallest independent state, covering less than half a square mile (44 hectares) in the center of Rome. Over half is garden, but the rest includes St. Peter's Basilica, St. Peter's Square, museums, and the Vatican palace. The Vatican is the home of the Pope, head of the Roman Catholic Church. Popes have lived in the Vatican since 1377, and they were the rulers of Rome and large parts of Italy for many centuries. Vatican City became an independent state in 1929, and has a population of about one thousand. Within its borders are some of the world's greatest works of art, such as Michelangelo's sculpture the *Pietà*, and his ceiling and wall paintings in the Sistine Chapel.

San Marino is the smallest republic in Europe and is situated in northeast Italy about 14 miles (23 kilometers) from Rimini on the Adriatic coast. It has an area of 23.5 square miles (61 square kilometers) and a population of about 23,000. The republic has maintained its independence since the 9th century and its constitution dates back to 1600. It began its history as a mountain stronghold to which early Christians, including St. Marinus, fled to avoid persecution in 301.

▼ Smoke often rises from the boiling lava within Mount Etna, but life carries on as usual around it.

Art and music

It has been estimated that two thirds of the historic monuments and works of art in the western world are Italian. The country has been robbed repeatedly for hundreds of years, yet it is still incredibly rich in important artistic works. No country has produced as many major artists and sculptors.

Italy has excelled in music also. The Italian air seems to inspire particularly outstanding singers, such as Enrico Caruso, Benjamino Gigli, and Luciano Pavarotti.

Grand opera is an Italian specialty, and one of the greatest and most popular composers of opera, Giuseppe Verdi, became a member of the first Italian government.

▼ The Ponte Vecchio across the River Arno in Florence has changed very little in the six hundred years since it was built.

What is an Italian?

Only since 1870 has modern Italy existed as a united country. For 1500 years before then it was divided into many parts: some large, some small, some under foreign control, some independent. Rivalry existed between the different regions. Because life was hard for many people, their loyalty had to be first to their family. Then they had loyalty to their birthplace. The state of ruling power commanded no loyalty, as it was often harsh in its treatment of the people. Italy as a concept did not exist.

To a great extent, these historical feelings of loyalty still remain. An Italian is first a member of his family, then a Roman, or a Florentine, or a Venetian. Only after that does he think of himself as an Italian.

B.C.	Time chart	1735-1806	Bourbons in Naples and Sicily.
2000-1800	Early Metal Age in northern Italy.	1768	Genoa sells Corsica to France.
1800-1000	Bronze Age in northern Italy.	1805	Napoleon becomes king of Italy.
1000-500	Villanovan culture near Bologna.		Liguria becomes part of France.
	The Etruscans from Asia Minor move to central Italy.	1816	Naples and Sicily united in the Kingdom of the Two Sicilies.
750-550	Greek colonies in Italy and Sicily.	1848-1849	Revolution in Italy and Sicily.
396-280	Rome conquers central Italy.	1860	Garibaldi and his "red shirts"
300-64	Roman rule extends to all Italy, Macedonia, Greece, Asia Minor.		conquer the Kingdom of the Two Sicilies in an effort to unite Italy
58-51	Julius Caesar conquers Gaul.		into one kingdom.
A.D.		1861	Victor Emmanuel the Second
14-395	Roman Empire reaches its greatest extent.		becomes king. First capital is Turin.
313	Constantine the Great grants religious freedom to Christians.	1866	War with Austria. Venice becomes part of Italy.
395	Division of Roman Empire into western and eastern parts.	1870	Rome becomes capital of Italy.
		1881	Alliance with Germany and
476	Last western Roman Emperor is deposed.		Austria-Hungary.
		1887-1896	War with Abyssinia.
800	Pope Leo III crowns Charlemagne Holy Roman Emperor.	1911-1912	War with Libya.
		1915-1918	Italy in World War One.
827	Saracens conquer Sicily.	1919	Italy receives South Tyrol.
899	Magyars plunder northern Italy.	1922	Benito Mussolini and Fascists take
951-1268	Italy ruled by German emperors; conflicts with the popes.		over government.
		1935-1936	Italians invade and take over
1000-1200	Southern Italy and Sicily become a Norman kingdom.		Abyssinia.
		1939	Occupation of Albania.
c.1041	World's first medical school at Salerno.	1940-1943	Italy fights against Allies in World War Two.
c.1060	University founded at Bologna.	1943	Fall of Fascist government. War
1250 on	Rise of independent city-states: Milan, Verona, Mantua, Venice, Genoa, Ferrara, Florence.		declared on Germany.
		1945	Mussolini is shot by partisans. End of World War Two.
1268-1442	Naples ruled by House of Anjou.	1946	Italy becomes a republic.
1282-1442	Sicily ruled by House of Aragon.	1960	Summer Olympic Games in Rome.
1504-1713	Sicily ruled by Spanish Habsburgs.	1966	Terrible floods in north and central Italy.
1703-1737	Mantua, Lombardy and Tuscany fall to Austria.	1980	Severe earthquake in southern Italy.
		1990	Soccer World Cup in Italy.

31

Index